MULTIPLICATION CHART

Directions: Complete this multiplication chart.

×	0	1	2	3	4	5	6	7	8	9	10
0	0					0					0
1		1				5				9	
2			4			10			16		
3				9		15		21			
4					16	20	24				
5	0	5	10	15	20	25	30	35	40	45	50
6					24	30	36				
7				21		35		49			
8			16			40			64		
9		9				45				81	
10	0										100

Skip Counting

Skip counting is the process of skipping numbers as counting occurs (e.g. 2, 4, 6...). Skip counting helps you to count numbers in a faster, more efficient way. It also begins the study of multiplication. Practice using the pictures below to help you skip count the different items on the page.

For example, you can count by twos to find out how many wings are on the page:

__2__   __2__   __2__ $(2 \times 3) =$ __6__ wings

Count by threes to figure out how many horns are on the page.

____ ____ ____ ____ $(3 \times 4) =$ ____ horns

Count by fives to figure out how many fingers are on the page.

____ ____ ____ $(5 \times 3) =$ ____ fingers

Skip Counting

Directions: Draw the pictures to match each sentence. Then count the total.

Example: 4 groups of cars with 3 in each group.

    = ______ cars

1. Draw 2 groups of stars with 4 in each group.

= ______ stars

2. Draw 3 groups of checkmarks with 4 in each group.

= ______ checkmarks

Directions: Use the drawings to fill in the blanks.

3. ______ groups of ______  = ______ trees

4. ______ groups of ______  = ______ fish

Multiplying by 0

Multiplying by 0 is easy. The product is always 0! Look at the examples.

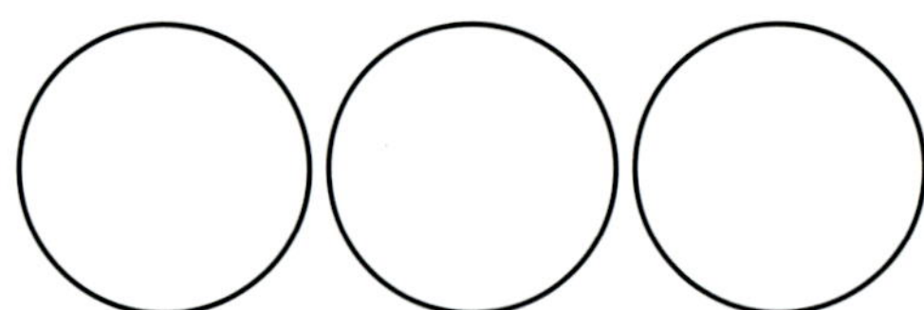

3 sets × 0 in each set = 0

3 × 0 = 0

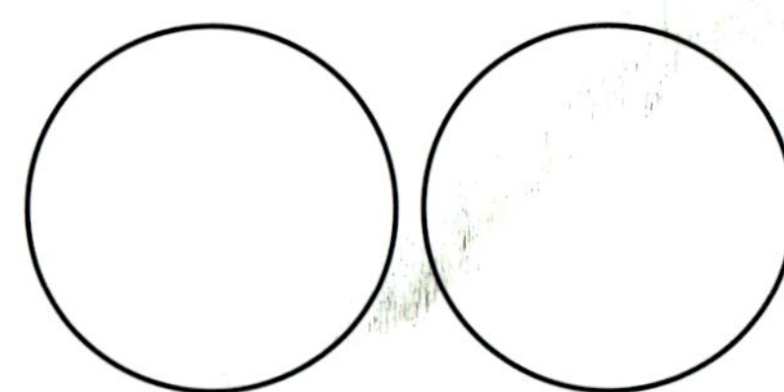

2 sets × 0 in each set = 0

2 × 0 = 0

Directions: Write the product to each problem on the line.

1. 10 × 0 = _____

2. 8 × 0 = _____

3. 0 × 0 = _____

4. 5 × 0 = _____

5. 0 × 3 = _____

6. 0 × 9 = _____

7. 2 × 0 = _____

8. 4 × 0 = _____

9. 11 × 0 = _____

10. 1 × 0 = _____

11. 6 × 0 = _____

12. 0 × 7 = _____

Practice!

Directions: Do these problems. See if you can do them in two minutes or less. Record your times below.

1. $\begin{array}{r} 5 \\ \times\ 0 \\ \hline \end{array}$	**2.** $\begin{array}{r} 0 \\ \times\ 2 \\ \hline \end{array}$	**3.** $\begin{array}{r} 6 \\ \times\ 0 \\ \hline \end{array}$	**4.** $\begin{array}{r} 0 \\ \times\ 1 \\ \hline \end{array}$	**5.** $\begin{array}{r} 7 \\ \times\ 0 \\ \hline \end{array}$
6. $\begin{array}{r} 0 \\ \times\ 3 \\ \hline \end{array}$	**7.** $\begin{array}{r} 10 \\ \times\ 0 \\ \hline \end{array}$	**8.** $\begin{array}{r} 0 \\ \times\ 0 \\ \hline \end{array}$	**9.** $\begin{array}{r} 9 \\ \times\ 0 \\ \hline \end{array}$	**10.** $\begin{array}{r} 0 \\ \times\ 8 \\ \hline \end{array}$
11. $\begin{array}{r} 11 \\ \times\ 0 \\ \hline \end{array}$	**12.** $\begin{array}{r} 0 \\ \times\ 7 \\ \hline \end{array}$	**13.** $\begin{array}{r} 12 \\ \times\ 0 \\ \hline \end{array}$	**14.** $\begin{array}{r} 0 \\ \times\ 6 \\ \hline \end{array}$	**15.** $\begin{array}{r} 1 \\ \times\ 0 \\ \hline \end{array}$
16. $\begin{array}{r} 8 \\ \times\ 0 \\ \hline \end{array}$	**17.** $\begin{array}{r} 0 \\ \times\ 3 \\ \hline \end{array}$	**18.** $\begin{array}{r} 0 \\ \times\ 10 \\ \hline \end{array}$	**19.** $\begin{array}{r} 4 \\ \times\ 0 \\ \hline \end{array}$	**20.** $\begin{array}{r} 0 \\ \times\ 12 \\ \hline \end{array}$

1ST TIME: __________   **2ND TIME:** __________   **BEST TIME:** __________

Multiplying by 1

Multiplying by 1 is also easy. The product is always the same as the other factor.

There is 1 set with 1 horse so the product is 1.

There are 2 sets with 1 goose in each set, and 2 is the other factor so the product is 2.

1 set × 1 horse in each set = 1 horse
1 × 1 = 1

2 sets × 1 goose in each set = 2 geese
2 × 1 = 2

Directions: Write the product of each problem on the line.

1. 7 × 1 = ______

2. 8 × 1 = ______

3. 6 × 1 = ______

4. 4 × 1 = ______

5. 1 × 9 = ______

6. 1 × 3 = ______

7. 10 × 1 = ______

8. 2 × 1 = ______

9. 5 × 1 = ______

10. 1 × 1 = ______

11. 0 × 1 = ______

12. 1 × 11 = ______

Practice! 

Directions: Do these problems. See if you can do them in two minutes or less.
Record your times below.

1. $\begin{array}{r} 1 \\ \times\ 0 \\ \hline \end{array}$	**2.** $\begin{array}{r} 3 \\ \times\ 1 \\ \hline \end{array}$	**3.** $\begin{array}{r} 5 \\ \times\ 1 \\ \hline \end{array}$	**4.** $\begin{array}{r} 1 \\ \times\ 1 \\ \hline \end{array}$	**5.** $\begin{array}{r} 10 \\ \times\ 1 \\ \hline \end{array}$
6. $\begin{array}{r} 1 \\ \times\ 6 \\ \hline \end{array}$	**7.** $\begin{array}{r} 4 \\ \times\ 1 \\ \hline \end{array}$	**8.** $\begin{array}{r} 1 \\ \times\ 2 \\ \hline \end{array}$	**9.** $\begin{array}{r} 8 \\ \times\ 1 \\ \hline \end{array}$	**10.** $\begin{array}{r} 1 \\ \times\ 9 \\ \hline \end{array}$
11. $\begin{array}{r} 12 \\ \times\ 1 \\ \hline \end{array}$	**12.** $\begin{array}{r} 1 \\ \times\ 3 \\ \hline \end{array}$	**13.** $\begin{array}{r} 2 \\ \times\ 1 \\ \hline \end{array}$	**14.** $\begin{array}{r} 1 \\ \times\ 11 \\ \hline \end{array}$	**15.** $\begin{array}{r} 1 \\ \times\ 7 \\ \hline \end{array}$
16. $\begin{array}{r} 9 \\ \times\ 1 \\ \hline \end{array}$	**17.** $\begin{array}{r} 1 \\ \times\ 6 \\ \hline \end{array}$	**18.** $\begin{array}{r} 1 \\ \times\ 10 \\ \hline \end{array}$	**19.** $\begin{array}{r} 5 \\ \times\ 1 \\ \hline \end{array}$	**20.** $\begin{array}{r} 1 \\ \times\ 8 \\ \hline \end{array}$

1ST TIME: _________   **2ND TIME:** _________   **BEST TIME:** _________

Multiplying by 2

The trick to multiplying by 2 is to remember that the product is simply the number plus itself!

There are 2 sets with 3 kites in each set.

$3 + 3 = 6$, which is the same as saying $2 \times 3 = 6$; the product is 6.

2 sets × 3 kites in each set = 6 kites

$$2 \times 3 = 6$$

Directions: Write the product of each problem on the line.

1. $10 \times 2 =$ _____

2. $8 \times 2 =$ _____

3. $0 \times 2 =$ _____

4. $5 \times 2 =$ _____

5. $2 \times 3 =$ _____

6. $2 \times 9 =$ _____

7. $2 \times 2 =$ _____

8. $4 \times 2 =$ _____

9. $12 \times 2 =$ _____

10. $1 \times 2 =$ _____

11. $6 \times 2 =$ _____

12. $2 \times 7 =$ _____

Directions: Do these problems. See if you can do them in two minutes or less. Record your times below.

1. $\begin{array}{r} 1 \\ \times\ 2 \\ \hline \end{array}$	**2.** $\begin{array}{r} 2 \\ \times\ 4 \\ \hline \end{array}$	**3.** $\begin{array}{r} 6 \\ \times\ 2 \\ \hline \end{array}$	**4.** $\begin{array}{r} 2 \\ \times\ 5 \\ \hline \end{array}$	**5.** $\begin{array}{r} 10 \\ \times\ 2 \\ \hline \end{array}$
6. $\begin{array}{r} 2 \\ \times\ 3 \\ \hline \end{array}$	**7.** $\begin{array}{r} 5 \\ \times\ 2 \\ \hline \end{array}$	**8.** $\begin{array}{r} 2 \\ \times\ 9 \\ \hline \end{array}$	**9.** $\begin{array}{r} 8 \\ \times\ 2 \\ \hline \end{array}$	**10.** $\begin{array}{r} 2 \\ \times\ 2 \\ \hline \end{array}$
11. $\begin{array}{r} 12 \\ \times\ 2 \\ \hline \end{array}$	**12.** $\begin{array}{r} 2 \\ \times\ 11 \\ \hline \end{array}$	**13.** $\begin{array}{r} 7 \\ \times\ 2 \\ \hline \end{array}$	**14.** $\begin{array}{r} 2 \\ \times\ 1 \\ \hline \end{array}$	**15.** $\begin{array}{r} 6 \\ \times\ 2 \\ \hline \end{array}$
16. $\begin{array}{r} 2 \\ \times\ 8 \\ \hline \end{array}$	**17.** $\begin{array}{r} 12 \\ \times\ 2 \\ \hline \end{array}$	**18.** $\begin{array}{r} 2 \\ \times\ 9 \\ \hline \end{array}$	**19.** $\begin{array}{r} 4 \\ \times\ 2 \\ \hline \end{array}$	**20.** $\begin{array}{r} 2 \\ \times\ 1 \\ \hline \end{array}$

1ST TIME: __________   **2ND TIME:** __________   **BEST TIME:** __________

Multiplying by 3

3 sets × 4 cows in each set = 12 cows

3 × 4 = 12

Directions: Write the product of each problem on the line.

1. 1 × 3 = _______

2. 6 × 3 = _______

3. 2 × 3 = _______

4. 5 × 3 = _______

5. 3 × 3 = _______

6. 3 × 11 = _______

7. 10 × 3 = _______

8. 9 × 3 = _______

9. 7 × 3 = _______

10. 4 × 3 = _______

11. 0 × 3 = _______

12. 3 × 8 = _______

Practice!

Directions: Do these problems. See if you can do them in two minutes or less. Record your times below.

1. $\begin{array}{r} 3 \\ \times\ 0 \\ \hline \end{array}$	**2.** $\begin{array}{r} 3 \\ \times\ 3 \\ \hline \end{array}$	**3.** $\begin{array}{r} 1 \\ \times\ 3 \\ \hline \end{array}$	**4.** $\begin{array}{r} 3 \\ \times\ 4 \\ \hline \end{array}$	**5.** $\begin{array}{r} 11 \\ \times\ 3 \\ \hline \end{array}$
6. $\begin{array}{r} 3 \\ \times\ 6 \\ \hline \end{array}$	**7.** $\begin{array}{r} 5 \\ \times\ 3 \\ \hline \end{array}$	**8.** $\begin{array}{r} 3 \\ \times\ 9 \\ \hline \end{array}$	**9.** $\begin{array}{r} 8 \\ \times\ 3 \\ \hline \end{array}$	**10.** $\begin{array}{r} 3 \\ \times\ 7 \\ \hline \end{array}$
11. $\begin{array}{r} 12 \\ \times\ 3 \\ \hline \end{array}$	**12.** $\begin{array}{r} 3 \\ \times\ 2 \\ \hline \end{array}$	**13.** $\begin{array}{r} 1 \\ \times\ 3 \\ \hline \end{array}$	**14.** $\begin{array}{r} 3 \\ \times\ 11 \\ \hline \end{array}$	**15.** $\begin{array}{r} 10 \\ \times\ 3 \\ \hline \end{array}$
16. $\begin{array}{r} 9 \\ \times\ 3 \\ \hline \end{array}$	**17.** $\begin{array}{r} 3 \\ \times\ 6 \\ \hline \end{array}$	**18.** $\begin{array}{r} 0 \\ \times\ 3 \\ \hline \end{array}$	**19.** $\begin{array}{r} 3 \\ \times\ 7 \\ \hline \end{array}$	**20.** $\begin{array}{r} 4 \\ \times\ 3 \\ \hline \end{array}$

1ST TIME: __________   **2ND TIME:** __________   **BEST TIME:** __________

Multiplying by 4

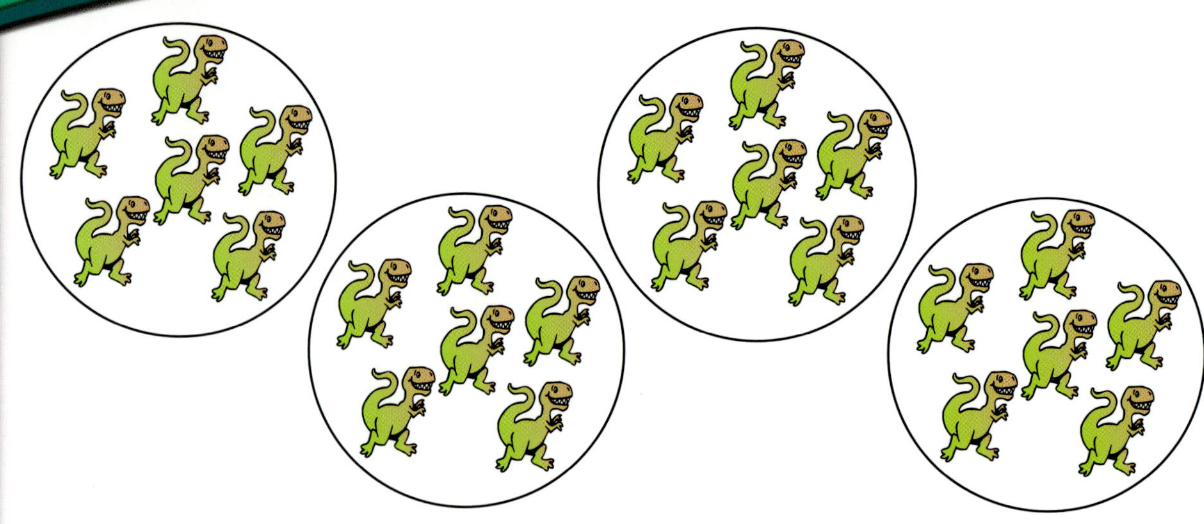

4 sets × 6 dinosaurs in each set = 24 dinosaurs

4 × 6 = 24

Directions: Write the product of each problem on the line.

1. 2 × 4 = ______

2. 6 × 4 = ______

3. 1 × 4 = ______

4. 0 × 4 = ______

5. 4 × 5 = ______

6. 4 × 9 = ______

7. 8 × 4 = ______

8. 10 × 4 = ______

9. 12 × 4 = ______

10. 7 × 4 = ______

11. 4 × 4 = ______

12. 4 × 3 = ______

Practice!

Directions: Do these problems. See if you can do them in two minutes or less. Record your times below.

1. 4 × 1	**2.** 2 × 4	**3.** 4 × 9	**4.** 7 × 4	**5.** 4 × 3
6. 4 × 6	**7.** 5 × 4	**8.** 4 × 10	**9.** 8 × 4	**10.** 4 × 12
11. 0 × 4	**12.** 4 × 2	**13.** 3 × 4	**14.** 4 × 11	**15.** 1 × 4
16. 4 × 7	**17.** 11 × 4	**18.** 4 × 4	**19.** 5 × 4	**20.** 4 × 6

1ST TIME: _________   **2ND TIME:** _________   **BEST TIME:** _________

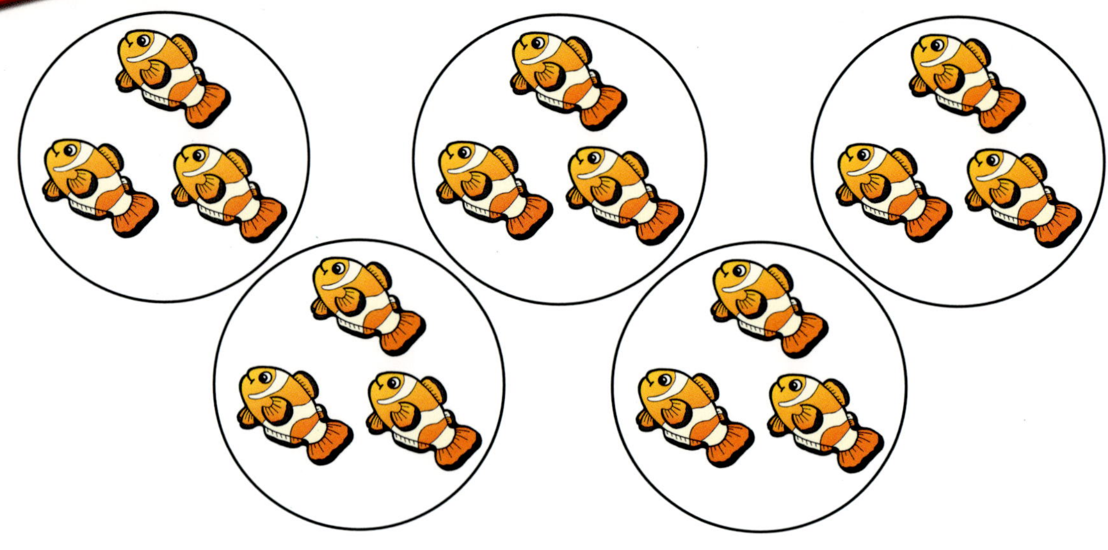

5 sets × 3 fish in each set = 15 fish

5 × 3 = 15

Directions: Write the product of each problem on the line.

1. 5 × 5 = ______

2. 3 × 5 = ______

3. 1 × 5 = ______

4. 8 × 5 = ______

5. 5 × 2 = ______

6. 5 × 7 = ______

7. 9 × 5 = ______

8. 10 × 5 = ______

9. 11 × 5 = ______

10. 0 × 5 = ______

11. 6 × 5 = ______

12. 5 × 4 = ______

Practice! 

Directions: Do these problems. See if you can do them in two minutes or less. Record your times below.

1. 5 × 5	**2.** 3 × 5	**3.** 5 × 1	**4.** 0 × 5	**5.** 5 × 4
6. 6 × 5	**7.** 5 × 7	**8.** 10 × 5	**9.** 5 × 9	**10.** 11 × 5
11. 5 × 12	**12.** 0 × 5	**13.** 5 × 9	**14.** 8 × 5	**15.** 5 × 7
16. 1 × 5	**17.** 5 × 3	**18.** 2 × 5	**19.** 5 × 4	**20.** 8 × 5

1ST TIME: _________   **2ND TIME:** _________   **BEST TIME:** _________

Multiplying by 6

6 sets × 8 cones in each set = 48 cones

6 × 8 = 48

Directions: Write the product of each problem on the line.

1. 1 × 6 = ______

2. 3 × 6 = ______

3. 2 × 6 = ______

4. 5 × 6 = ______

5. 6 × 4 = ______

6. 6 × 7 = ______

7. 0 × 6 = ______

8. 10 × 6 = ______

9. 6 × 6 = ______

10. 8 × 6 = ______

11. 6 × 9 = ______

12. 6 × 11 = ______

Practice! 

Directions: Do these problems. See if you can do them in two minutes or less. Record your times below.

1. $\begin{array}{r} 6 \\ \times\ 2 \\ \hline \end{array}$	**2.** $\begin{array}{r} 7 \\ \times\ 6 \\ \hline \end{array}$	**3.** $\begin{array}{r} 6 \\ \times\ 4 \\ \hline \end{array}$	**4.** $\begin{array}{r} 0 \\ \times\ 6 \\ \hline \end{array}$	**5.** $\begin{array}{r} 6 \\ \times\ 1 \\ \hline \end{array}$
6. $\begin{array}{r} 12 \\ \times\ 6 \\ \hline \end{array}$	**7.** $\begin{array}{r} 6 \\ \times\ 11 \\ \hline \end{array}$	**8.** $\begin{array}{r} 5 \\ \times\ 6 \\ \hline \end{array}$	**9.** $\begin{array}{r} 6 \\ \times\ 3 \\ \hline \end{array}$	**10.** $\begin{array}{r} 6 \\ \times\ 6 \\ \hline \end{array}$
11. $\begin{array}{r} 6 \\ \times\ 8 \\ \hline \end{array}$	**12.** $\begin{array}{r} 10 \\ \times\ 6 \\ \hline \end{array}$	**13.** $\begin{array}{r} 6 \\ \times\ 2 \\ \hline \end{array}$	**14.** $\begin{array}{r} 5 \\ \times\ 6 \\ \hline \end{array}$	**15.** $\begin{array}{r} 6 \\ \times\ 11 \\ \hline \end{array}$
16. $\begin{array}{r} 7 \\ \times\ 6 \\ \hline \end{array}$	**17.** $\begin{array}{r} 6 \\ \times\ 9 \\ \hline \end{array}$	**18.** $\begin{array}{r} 1 \\ \times\ 6 \\ \hline \end{array}$	**19.** $\begin{array}{r} 6 \\ \times\ 12 \\ \hline \end{array}$	**20.** $\begin{array}{r} 3 \\ \times\ 6 \\ \hline \end{array}$

1ST TIME: __________   **2ND TIME:** __________   **BEST TIME:** __________

Multiplying by 7

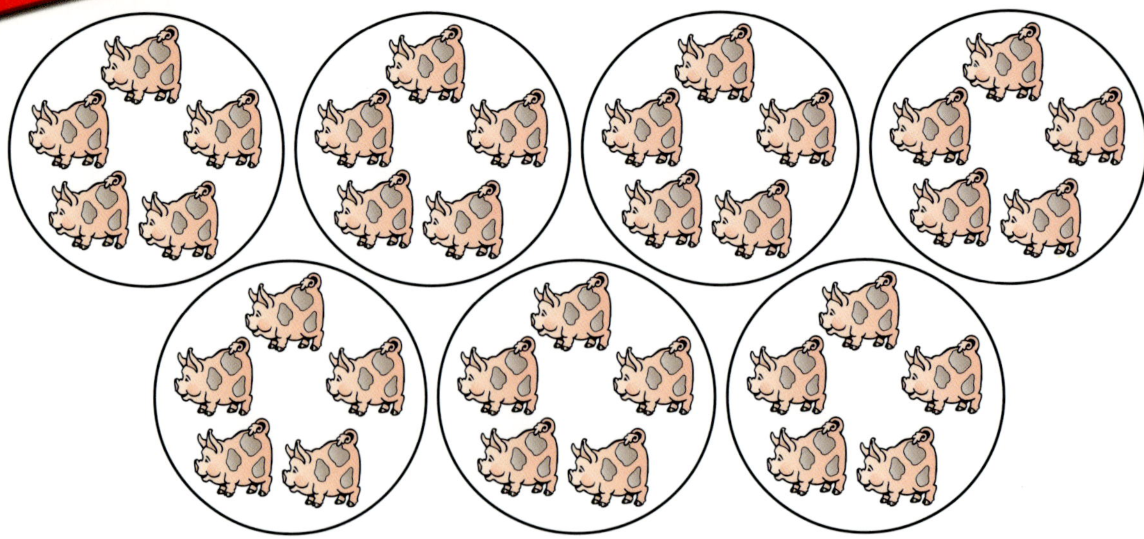

7 sets × 5 pigs in each set = 35 pigs

7 × 5 = 35

Directions: Write the product of each problem on the line.

1. 10 × 7 = _____

2. 1 × 7 = _____

3. 4 × 7 = _____

4. 5 × 7 = _____

5. 7 × 2 = _____

6. 7 × 9 = _____

7. 8 × 7 = _____

8. 3 × 7 = _____

9. 11 × 7 = _____

10. 0 × 7 = _____

11. 6 × 7 = _____

12. 7 × 7 = _____

Practice!

Directions: Do these problems. See if you can do them in two minutes or less. Record your times below.

1. $\begin{array}{r} 7 \\ \times\ 0 \\ \hline \end{array}$	**2.** $\begin{array}{r} 2 \\ \times\ 7 \\ \hline \end{array}$	**3.** $\begin{array}{r} 7 \\ \times\ 1 \\ \hline \end{array}$	**4.** $\begin{array}{r} 3 \\ \times\ 7 \\ \hline \end{array}$	**5.** $\begin{array}{r} 7 \\ \times\ 7 \\ \hline \end{array}$
6. $\begin{array}{r} 6 \\ \times\ 7 \\ \hline \end{array}$	**7.** $\begin{array}{r} 7 \\ \times\ 4 \\ \hline \end{array}$	**8.** $\begin{array}{r} 8 \\ \times\ 7 \\ \hline \end{array}$	**9.** $\begin{array}{r} 7 \\ \times\ 10 \\ \hline \end{array}$	**10.** $\begin{array}{r} 5 \\ \times\ 7 \\ \hline \end{array}$
11. $\begin{array}{r} 7 \\ \times\ 9 \\ \hline \end{array}$	**12.** $\begin{array}{r} 12 \\ \times\ 7 \\ \hline \end{array}$	**13.** $\begin{array}{r} 7 \\ \times\ 2 \\ \hline \end{array}$	**14.** $\begin{array}{r} 11 \\ \times\ 7 \\ \hline \end{array}$	**15.** $\begin{array}{r} 7 \\ \times\ 4 \\ \hline \end{array}$
16. $\begin{array}{r} 5 \\ \times\ 7 \\ \hline \end{array}$	**17.** $\begin{array}{r} 7 \\ \times\ 9 \\ \hline \end{array}$	**18.** $\begin{array}{r} 7 \\ \times\ 7 \\ \hline \end{array}$	**19.** $\begin{array}{r} 7 \\ \times\ 10 \\ \hline \end{array}$	**20.** $\begin{array}{r} 6 \\ \times\ 7 \\ \hline \end{array}$

1ST TIME: __________   **2ND TIME:** __________   **BEST TIME:** __________

Multiplying by 8

8 sets × 7 bananas in each set = 56 bananas

8 × 7 = 56

Directions: Write the product of each problem on the line.

1. 10 × 8 = ______

2. 6 × 8 = ______

3. 11 × 8 = ______

4. 5 × 8 = ______

5. 8 × 7 = ______

6. 8 × 0 = ______

7. 2 × 8 = ______

8. 4 × 8 = ______

9. 3 × 8 = ______

10. 1 × 8 = ______

11. 8 × 8 = ______

12. 8 × 9 = ______

Practice!

Directions: Do these problems. See if you can do them in two minutes or less. Record your times below.

1. 8 × 4	**2.** 8 × 8	**3.** 8 × 2	**4.** 0 × 8	**5.** 8 × 6
6. 12 × 8	**7.** 8 × 9	**8.** 3 × 8	**9.** 8 × 7	**10.** 11 × 8
11. 8 × 10	**12.** 5 × 8	**13.** 8 × 7	**14.** 12 × 8	**15.** 8 × 0
16. 9 × 8	**17.** 8 × 6	**18.** 10 × 8	**19.** 8 × 4	**20.** 1 × 8

1ST TIME: __________   **2ND TIME:** __________   **BEST TIME:** __________

Multiplying by 9

9 sets × 4 stars in each set = 36 stars

9 × 4 = 36

Directions: Write the product of each problem on the line.

1. 1 × 9 = ______

2. 11 × 9 = ______

3. 2 × 9 = ______

4. 5 × 9 = ______

5. 9 × 10 = ______

6. 9 × 12 = ______

7. 3 × 9 = ______

8. 9 × 9 = ______

9. 4 × 9 = ______

10. 8 × 9 = ______

11. 6 × 9 = ______

12. 9 × 7 = ______

Practice!

Directions: Do these problems. See if you can do them in two minutes or less. Record your times below.

1. 9 × 0	**2.** 2 × 9	**3.** 9 × 4	**4.** 1 × 9	**5.** 9 × 6
6. 9 × 9	**7.** 9 × 12	**8.** 8 × 9	**9.** 9 × 3	**10.** 5 × 9
11. 9 × 10	**12.** 4 × 9	**13.** 9 × 0	**14.** 11 × 9	**15.** 9 × 1
16. 6 × 9	**17.** 9 × 8	**18.** 7 × 9	**19.** 9 × 3	**20.** 12 × 9

1st Time: __________ **2nd Time:** __________ **Best Time:** __________

Multiplying by 10

10 sets × 3 socks in each set = 30 socks

10 × 3 = 30

Directions: Write the product of each problem on the line.

1. 3 × 10 = _______

2. 8 × 10 = _______

3. 0 × 10 = _______

4. 1 × 10 = _______

5. 10 × 2 = _______

6. 10 × 5 = _______

7. 10 × 10 = _______

8. 11 × 10 = _______

9. 4 × 10 = _______

10. 6 × 10 = _______

11. 7 × 10 = _______

12. 10 × 9 = _______

Practice!

Directions: Do these problems. See if you can do them in two minutes or less. Record your times below.

1. 10 × 0	**2.** 3 × 10	**3.** 5 × 10	**4.** 1 × 10	**5.** 10 × 10
6. 10 × 6	**7.** 4 × 10	**8.** 10 × 9	**9.** 7 × 10	**10.** 10 × 8
11. 12 × 10	**12.** 10 × 4	**13.** 2 × 10	**14.** 10 × 11	**15.** 9 × 10
16. 7 × 10	**17.** 10 × 8	**18.** 4 × 10	**19.** 10 × 12	**20.** 10 × 10

1ST TIME: _________   **2ND TIME:** _________   **BEST TIME:** _________

Multiplying by 11

11 sets × 3 feathers in each set = 33 feathers

11 × 3 = 33

Directions: Write the product of each problem on the line.

1. 1 × 11 = _______

2. 10 × 11 = _______

3. 0 × 11 = _______

4. 7 × 11 = _______

5. 11 × 11 = _______

6. 11 × 9 = _______

7. 4 × 11 = _______

8. 2 × 11 = _______

9. 3 × 11 = _______

10. 5 × 11 = _______

11. 6 × 11 = _______

12. 11 × 8 = _______

Practice! 

Directions: Do these problems. See if you can do them in two minutes or less. Record your times below.

1. $\begin{array}{r} 11 \\ \times\ 10 \\ \hline \end{array}$	**2.** $\begin{array}{r} 3 \\ \times\ 11 \\ \hline \end{array}$	**3.** $\begin{array}{r} 11 \\ \times\ 11 \\ \hline \end{array}$	**4.** $\begin{array}{r} 5 \\ \times\ 11 \\ \hline \end{array}$	**5.** $\begin{array}{r} 11 \\ \times\ 7 \\ \hline \end{array}$
6. $\begin{array}{r} 11 \\ \times\ 1 \\ \hline \end{array}$	**7.** $\begin{array}{r} 4 \\ \times\ 11 \\ \hline \end{array}$	**8.** $\begin{array}{r} 11 \\ \times\ 7 \\ \hline \end{array}$	**9.** $\begin{array}{r} 8 \\ \times\ 11 \\ \hline \end{array}$	**10.** $\begin{array}{r} 11 \\ \times\ 12 \\ \hline \end{array}$
11. $\begin{array}{r} 9 \\ \times\ 11 \\ \hline \end{array}$	**12.** $\begin{array}{r} 11 \\ \times\ 10 \\ \hline \end{array}$	**13.** $\begin{array}{r} 0 \\ \times\ 11 \\ \hline \end{array}$	**14.** $\begin{array}{r} 11 \\ \times\ 2 \\ \hline \end{array}$	**15.** $\begin{array}{r} 4 \\ \times\ 11 \\ \hline \end{array}$
16. $\begin{array}{r} 6 \\ \times\ 11 \\ \hline \end{array}$	**17.** $\begin{array}{r} 11 \\ \times\ 9 \\ \hline \end{array}$	**18.** $\begin{array}{r} 8 \\ \times\ 11 \\ \hline \end{array}$	**19.** $\begin{array}{r} 11 \\ \times\ 12 \\ \hline \end{array}$	**20.** $\begin{array}{r} 11 \\ \times\ 11 \\ \hline \end{array}$

1ST TIME: __________   **2ND TIME:** __________   **BEST TIME:** __________

Multiplying by 12

12 sets × 2 crayons in each set = 24 crayons

12 × 2 = 24

Directions: Write the product of each problem on the line.

1. $0 \times 12 =$ _____

2. $11 \times 12 =$ _____

3. $10 \times 12 =$ _____

4. $12 \times 12 =$ _____

5. $12 \times 2 =$ _____

6. $12 \times 9 =$ _____

7. $8 \times 12 =$ _____

8. $5 \times 12 =$ _____

9. $3 \times 12 =$ _____

10. $4 \times 12 =$ _____

11. $7 \times 12 =$ _____

12. $12 \times 6 =$ _____

Practice! 

Directions: Do these problems. See if you can do them in two minutes or less. Record your times below.

1. 12 × 0	**2.** 3 × 12	**3.** 12 × 1	**4.** 5 × 12	**5.** 12 × 9
6. 12 × 6	**7.** 4 × 12	**8.** 12 × 2	**9.** 8 × 12	**10.** 12 × 10
11. 12 × 12	**12.** 12 × 6	**13.** 2 × 12	**14.** 12 × 11	**15.** 1 × 12
16. 9 × 12	**17.** 12 × 7	**18.** 8 × 12	**19.** 12 × 10	**20.** 12 × 12

1ST TIME: __________   **2ND TIME:** __________   **BEST TIME:** __________

Timed Test 1

Directions: Try to solve all these problems in two minutes or less.

1. 8 × 4	**2.** 7 × 3	**3.** 4 × 12	**4.** 10 × 9	**5.** 5 × 8
6. 9 × 11	**7.** 7 × 6	**8.** 6 × 5	**9.** 4 × 10	**10.** 12 × 4
11. 5 × 9	**12.** 3 × 8	**13.** 12 × 9	**14.** 8 × 8	**15.** 9 × 9
16. 5 × 2	**17.** 3 × 11	**18.** 9 × 2	**19.** 8 × 0	**20.** 6 × 11

1ST TIME: _________   **2ND TIME:** _________   **BEST TIME:** _________

Timed Test 2

Directions: Try to solve all these problems in two minutes or less.

1. 9×8	**2.** 4×7	**3.** 10×12	**4.** 11×2	**5.** 3×5
6. 5×0	**7.** 9×4	**8.** 10×1	**9.** 9×9	**10.** 3×12
11. 6×2	**12.** 8×0	**13.** 1×3	**14.** 5×5	**15.** 8×7
16. 4×12	**17.** 0×11	**18.** 2×10	**19.** 8×4	**20.** 1×7

1ST TIME: __________ **2ND TIME:** __________ **BEST TIME:** __________

Answer Key

Page 1

×	0	1	2	3	4	5	6	7	8	9	10
0	0	0	0	0	0	0	0	0	0	0	0
1	0	1	2	3	4	5	6	7	8	9	10
2	0	2	4	6	8	10	12	14	16	18	20
3	0	3	6	9	12	15	18	21	24	27	30
4	0	4	8	12	16	20	24	28	32	36	40
5	0	5	10	15	20	25	30	35	40	45	50
6	0	6	12	18	24	30	36	42	48	54	60
7	0	7	14	21	28	35	42	49	56	63	70
8	0	8	16	24	32	40	48	56	64	72	80
9	0	9	18	27	36	45	54	63	72	81	90
10	0	10	20	30	40	50	60	70	80	90	100

Page 2

12 horns
15 fingers

Page 3

12 cars

1. 8 stars
2. 12 checkmarks
3. 2 groups of 2; 4 trees
4. 4 groups of 4; 16 fish

Page 4

1.–12. 0

Page 5

1.–20. 0

Page 6

1. 7
2. 8
3. 6
4. 4
5. 9
6. 3
7. 10
8. 2
9. 5
10. 1
11. 0
12. 11

Page 7

1. 0
2. 3
3. 5
4. 1
5. 10
6. 6
7. 4
8. 2
9. 8
10. 9
11. 12
12. 3
13. 2
14. 11
15. 7
16. 9
17. 6
18. 10
19. 5
20. 8

Page 8

1. 20
2. 16
3. 0
4. 10
5. 6
6. 18
7. 4
8. 8
9. 24
10. 2
11. 12
12. 14

Page 9

1. 2
2. 8
3. 12
4. 10
5. 20
6. 6
7. 10
8. 18
9. 16
10. 4
11. 24
12. 22
13. 14
14. 2
15. 12
16. 16
17. 24
18. 18
19. 8
20. 2

Page 10

1. 3
2. 18
3. 6
4. 15
5. 9
6. 33
7. 30
8. 27
9. 21
10. 12
11. 0
12. 24

Page 11

1. 0
2. 9
3. 3
4. 12
5. 33
6. 18
7. 15
8. 27
9. 24
10. 21
11. 36
12. 6
13. 3
14. 33
15. 30
16. 27
17. 18
18. 0
19. 21
20. 12

Page 12

1. 8
2. 24
3. 4
4. 0
5. 20
6. 36
7. 32
8. 40
9. 48
10. 28
11. 16
12. 12

Page 13

1. 4
2. 8
3. 36
4. 28
5. 12
6. 24
7. 20
8. 40
9. 32
10. 48
11. 0
12. 8
13. 12
14. 44
15. 4
16. 28
17. 44
18. 16
19. 20
20. 24

Page 14

1. 25
2. 15
3. 5
4. 40
5. 10
6. 35
7. 45
8. 50
9. 55
10. 0
11. 30
12. 20

Page 15

1. 25
2. 15
3. 5
4. 0
5. 20
6. 30
7. 35
8. 50
9. 45
10. 55
11. 60
12. 0
13. 45
14. 40
15. 35
16. 5
17. 15
18. 10
19. 20
20. 40

Page 16

1. 6
2. 18
3. 12
4. 30
5. 24
6. 42
7. 0
8. 60
9. 36
10. 48
11. 54
12. 66

Page 17

1. 12
2. 42
3. 24
4. 0
5. 6
6. 72
7. 66
8. 30
9. 18
10. 36
11. 48
12. 60
13. 12
14. 30
15. 66
16. 42
17. 54
18. 6
19. 72
20. 18

Page 18

1. 70
2. 7
3. 28
4. 35
5. 14
6. 63
7. 56
8. 21
9. 77
10. 0
11. 42
12. 49

Page 19

1. 0
2. 14
3. 7
4. 21
5. 49
6. 42
7. 28
8. 56
9. 70
10. 35
11. 63
12. 84
13. 14
14. 77
15. 28
16. 35
17. 63
18. 49
19. 70
20. 42

Page 20

1. 80
2. 48
3. 88
4. 40
5. 56
6. 0
7. 16
8. 32
9. 24
10. 8
11. 64
12. 72

Page 21

1. 32
2. 64
3. 16
4. 0
5. 48
6. 96
7. 72
8. 24
9. 56
10. 88
11. 80
12. 40
13. 56
14. 96
15. 35
16. 72
17. 48
18. 80
19. 32
20. 8

Page 22

1. 9
2. 99
3. 18
4. 45
5. 90
6. 108
7. 27
8. 81
9. 36
10. 72
11. 54
12. 63

Page 23

1. 0
2. 18
3. 36
4. 9
5. 54
6. 81
7. 108
8. 72
9. 27
10. 45
11. 90
12. 36
13. 0
14. 99
15. 9
16. 54
17. 72
18. 63
19. 27
20. 108

Page 24

1. 30
2. 80
3. 0
4. 10
5. 20
6. 50
7. 100
8. 110
9. 40
10. 60
11. 70
12. 90

Page 25

1. 0
2. 30
3. 50
4. 10
5. 100
6. 60
7. 40
8. 90
9. 70
10. 80
11. 120
12. 40
13. 20
14. 110
15. 90
16. 70
17. 80
18. 40
19. 120
20. 100

Page 26

1. 11
2. 110
3. 0
4. 77
5. 121
6. 99
7. 44
8. 22
9. 24
10. 55
11. 66
12. 88

Page 27

1. 110
2. 33
3. 121
4. 55
5. 77
6. 11
7. 44
8. 77
9. 88
10. 132
11. 99
12. 110
13. 0
14. 22
15. 44
16. 66
17. 99
18. 88
19. 132
20. 121

Page 28

1. 0
2. 132
3. 120
4. 144
5. 24
6. 108
7. 96
8. 60
9. 36
10. 48
11. 84
12. 72

Page 29

1. 0
2. 36
3. 12
4. 60
5. 108
6. 72
7. 48
8. 24
9. 96
10. 120
11. 144
12. 72
13. 24
14. 132
15. 12
16. 108
17. 84
18. 96
19. 120
20. 144

Page 30

1. 32
2. 21
3. 48
4. 90
5. 40
6. 99
7. 42
8. 30
9. 40
10. 48
11. 45
12. 24
13. 108
14. 64
15. 81
16. 10
17. 33
18. 18
19. 0
20. 66

Page 31

1. 72
2. 28
3. 120
4. 22
5. 15
6. 0
7. 36
8. 10
9. 81
10. 36
11. 12
12. 0
13. 3
14. 25
15. 56
16. 48
17. 0
18. 20
19. 32
20. 7